Simple With

David Appelbaum

ISBN: 978-81-19228-14-0

First Edition: 2023
Rs. 200/-

Cyberwit.net
HIG 45 Kaushambi Kunj, Kalindipuram
Allahabad - 211011 (U.P.) India
http://www.cyberwit.net
Tel: +(91) 9415091004
E-mail: info@cyberwit.net

Printed at Vcore LLP.

Contents

The cure 5
Reception 6
Footprints 7
Horizon 8
Ads 9
The cap 10
This life 11
Repeat 12
Text 13
What is 14
Hearken, Alice 15
Choice 16
The puzzle 17
Compass, beware. 18
Without music 19
Prompts 20
Make-work 21
Multiple personalities 22
Renamed 23
Picayune 24
Cerberus 25
Advice 26
Birdsong 27
Gaming 28
Speech 29
Chance 30
Nerves 32
Spring 33
Song 34
Dystopia 35
Illusion 36

Illumination 37
Agility 38
Eastward 39
Longing 40
Twice 41
As if to say 43
Competition 44
On planning 45
Boxed in 46
Blasphemy 47
Morning 48
The window back 49
Ground zero 50
A shot in the dark 51
The call 52
The splash 53
Counsel 54
Verdict 55
Message 56
Autumn 57
Solution 58
Rescue 59
Prescience 60
Faith 61
Medley 63
Danse 65
Care-giving 66
Reproduction 67
On tour 68
In praise 69
Afterlife 70
Getaway 71
Duotrope 72
Artistry 73
The news 74

The cure

blight curls the rose bush
pinholes in veins

the thing doused white
'cure worse than the disease'

what can I say to make
things better?

last night I gave up writing,
seeing words I'd written

had no thorns

'leaves' instead of 'bush'?

Reception

an iris pretends to have
flopped-over rabbit ears

like an old TV antenna
fireflies take for real

it won't help the drought
that turns life into dust

a bud once impacted
wants to bolt next week

check the weather map's
glittery image

heat wave in full color
this, a few satellite beeps
on a tin foil aerial

Footprints

tracking
like tap dance
is sometimes difficult
to follow

a tang
(like lemon chai)
fades

in some obscure mailbox
in New Jersey
where passion calls
to cry and deny

suspicion:
the object hasn't been
itself lately
unwilling to exist

it may subtend
a range
of alternative times
call it scam

Horizon

a small event
spider web touches my face
in the dark

like evidence in a dream
dissolves
as I ask, what is it?

while unborn arachnid
generations
blink out like stars too

whose event-strings
puffs and dashes
of cosmic code

karmically connected
to that frail weaver
collapse

a wait renewed
will abort a future
of glad tidings

a crimped horizon
bent broken back by
a thread of annoyance

Ads

trash talk borders on
language reform

likewise, concave mirrors
vet a new look of you

I'm a sucker for found art
old masters need a break

we'll have time for parodies
to catch and rank them

in syndicated ripples
far sides of one trend

insane mirror events
jointed to one another

at the supermarket
rice cereal mimes wheat

is it like that where you are?

The cap

a ripe tomato wears
a crown of gauzy white mold

something is going around

referring to special ills
that implicate you

the passage signified—
senescence—

you don't get it
until you have it

(always pre-owned)

having arisen effortlessly
without sensation

the mind's wild haunt
splits as you look

red crowing yellow seeds

it's your story of
personal existence

but really the fact is
summer heat drives mildew

This life

my rest mass
is tugging on
‘what if’

the elastic
of the rubber band
is fatigued,
doesn’t stretch
actuality

I’m stuck
being essentially
what I am
by default

put that way
it’s as if I’m making
some mistake
by living

Repeat

continuous repetition
like sleep learning

causes a wobble
in the brain

as it misses the tipping point
once and for all

the worried dullness
of a dial tone

now a pointy cursor
arming an internet screen

passions are nothing at all
while doubtful asides

rage with self-criticism
about the missing link

again and again and again

Text

go to 30330
what you glean is
click here
key those numbers

walk three blocks
take a left . . .

drive south
find correct zip

sit on the sofa
left three, enter
right three, etc.

getting ‘to’ is strange
when where
is not a decent place

What is

faster than light
can jump
over your own knees

a dystopic thought
like hemorrhagic divers
where our cities

wink out one
by one from
excessive speed

between the quick
and the dead's
unnatural dilemma

the furies face—
Clotho and Lachesis—
since destiny

there waits before
your eyes meet
the first day's

forward speed

Hearken, Alice

a misaligned rug
ruffles and waves
so as to seem beautiful

at a singular cost
accomplishes
'risk of falling'

trailblazing
with hesitant steps
as if indecisive

to play beside aisles
with rabbit holes
to fall into

who needs a safari guide—
the treacle pool below is
a zoologist's dream

Choice

rumbling reservations
say 'I'

as if dark matter
tweaked a voice

to freight your choices
with mock distress

ghosts never are
fully dead

nor zombie inhabitants
of every 'yes'

while dewdrops dried
with noon-ish wind

sough real vagaries
like 'you shouldn't'

The puzzle

small white flies
congregate
a black sheet of paper

herald to the next
connect-the-dots
puzzle

they find the mind
thinks in swerves
to avoid collision

with itself
its denial of
the big picture

but subsequent editions
offer
a glob of honey

a tiff of saccharine
to allay
circumspection

Compass, beware.

tiny black flies
flock to my wine glass

iron filings would dream
of a dancing pole

the way lovers might
in conjunction

mutual containment
is the same act

only now magnetic north
is on the prowl

loping toward Siberia
possibly Irkutsk

loopy metal with
a drunken death wish

daring me to quaff it
in a single gulp

Without music

a storm left the sky
orange as a life
preserver

with a single contrail
to tie it
around my waist

but when I ducked down
to pull it over
my head

water plugged my ears
my voice called out
'Enough. No, *more.*'

Prompts

upside down
prompts
a slough
that hangs in
a banana tree
to stand downside up

an inverted image
holds a mirror
to the prompt
so that opposites
can neuter
the difference:

let it go

Make-work

bad beach day
wind is a music
wet leaves dance

is quiet rain
to drip in
cacophony?

is 'rain' to
replace 'wind'
in the phoneme

is 'bad' too
singular
an attitude

is 'dance'
a word too small
to fit?

Multiple personalities

yellow leaves
stepping stones
across tarmac

in a millipede's eyes
continents adrift

with persistent desire
larboard
as first frost's

prophecies
of grey death

while I
in the first person
stand stock-still

believing myself
a butterfly
trapped in my flesh

unable to take
the first step

toward flight

Renamed

the sage has risen

who can say that?

thank goodness for
homophony

it rocks the ocean
and grinds metal waves

in confusion

two words
same round

I only meant
the herb

planted last spring
is thriving.

Picayune

now the world is different

our incensed vigil
over name-changes

even the smallest
most under-rated

like the dots of an 'i'
or a 'j'

is an endangered species

each and every tittle
reminds us of something

like our lack of any
real depth-of-being

Cerberus

at bottom
the sun's hang dog
morning face

beams outward
like dark energy
once trapped
in its own gravitas

do try
take a left at zero
to rejoin
your inner bloodhound

for the scent
of dank tunnels
in and through which
the loving crank steals

Advice

a pinky ring
for the minimus

my grandfather's
had a mood stone

the future, he said
is around us, grimly

the color was
cerulean

beware, he said
the Judas kiss

the color was
cadmium

he found it
in a Cracker Jacks

where he learned
to feign prophecy

Birdsong

the tit tit
of the catbird

like the ting ting
of my cell phone

circles hope
at escape velocity

bouncing phonemes
off the brain

of the predator/
creditor

as if a story
could slow extinction

but then then then then's
a storyteller stutter

Gaming

wind like the bishop
on the chessboard

tells truth
but tells it slant

a medieval dance
double-jointed

rakes the pawns
who will fluidity

to the gambit

so corn is king
and king is king

and unction ready
for the final mate

Speech

a spry squiggle
of light on the screen
is called sun

it likes to move
like a moth
thrumming wings

when wind howls
it goes to the flame

eye scanning
is a valuable aid
to the cosmos

when blessed by
visemes
lip-round vowels

Chance

green is tinted down
on the register

a straw vote
on early take-outs

much is up in the air

as shrived privet leaves
cast sumptuous shade

to mask contingency

the bounce of one
atom off another

might end you in a hole

looking up at the
impossible stars

an astrologer who bets
on soy beans

or the one who said
eureka!

as he saw glory
in his well hole

black vault
a collar

Nerves

topsy turvy

the given knows
your refusal

since greed
is law
desire brays

it's dumb to be
gifted

meaning, too easy
on yourself

tired of negating
the no

relax, bend down
look between your legs—

the sun also rises
bigger than ever

seen downside up
upside down

Spring

seasonal creep
is setting
its arthritic pace

no equinoctial leap
no crisp dismissal
of by-gones

no first rush
of enthusiasm—
now just a grudge

a *schmear*
without distinction

how will I know
when to put
the woolens away?

Song

morning twangs
on the chromatic scale
right below hoots

swatches show up
on felt
as if display was

tissue-thin leaves

end-splitting
the difference—
suave streaks

spikes from branches
prismed out—
God's sunlight.

Dystopia

summer plants droop
high on thirst

white is out of fashion

the difference of
de rigueur and optional

weed tops wormy seedy
stalks of grain

worry a future

how far it will
dissemble

whether we will be
stomping toxic dust

antidote
to our best hope?

Illusion

curtains
meaning *the end*
unfolds folds
over the lake

unrulily
ruling this dawn
a graceful
wobble

as if to screen
a parting
image

an artist
surprise—
the *purdah*

its womanly self
'is the crafted
illusion'

Illumination

flip a switch

in sudden metaphor
desire flickers
sinks down flares
up

it reveres
a deep throb

unlike recognition
which is light
stippled names

cut to the quick

as mice scatter
in fluid motion
before freezing into
the shape

of what they are—
animal desire

Agility

somersault

some kind twist
inverts

down and outside
in

perfectly
in flight

both ways at once
go nowhere

but land
ball-footed

catching late sun

Eastward

smothered light
as crystal bells fling
with the sun
a hook-up

one hour before rain

a web survives
to wish for more
solace on waking

spiders dawn
like trolls
scamper to dodge
ossifying beams

as do I a current
in the ocean
that pushes
beyond slotted lands

a dark recoil
behind
the horizon waits

Longing

rocks on the railing
look crotchety

their view astonishing
leagues of sea

suffering its own
deflection

pallid clouds
a short chin

flaccid waves
seek your approval

none of the stoic
granite

holds its ground
under heart swells

seizure of mood
dramatic partings

inconstantly
prostrate

to your immortality

Twice

the irony of mirrors
doubles everything

things of two suns
two moons

twin loves twin
hates twin

approving thoughts
are twice as many
as before

but 'before' also has
Siamese
in time

new math
but to be invested

to get a handle
on the menagerie

to halve things
heal double vision

scratch second sight

forget two heads
are better than

one

As if to say

small birds pop like seeds
out of a dahlia

a keening wind cuts
like a knife

spewing metamemes
splaying misnomers

dust complains
we cannot see

I say, seen any whales
when one breaches

is that an example
of clarity?

Competition

nine rain-wet rocks
gleam under nine
morning suns
each looking best
in profile

an unbidden rival
garners praise

not of beauty
or radiance

but eloquent
choice of socks

bids in hyphens

a—a

On planning

right for all the wrong
reasons
it's a horse race

when logic gets tied
double-jointedly

into knotted intervals
to pretend nobody

has to kowtow to choice
in a big way
just show off a new

rug in an empty room
behind a velvet rope

God in white script

a background
that for now can
safely be ignored

Boxed in

to fill a blank
under the nib

script's well-being
in feeling out
an environment

words have to
have clout to

catch us where
we are today

right or wrong
free or stuck

which is why
I like photons'

simple ergs of
energy

Blasphemy

a fly
on the man's forehead

stayed
the demagoguery

to entice a certain
name and shape to mind

(Beelzebub
in fact)

with power
to shape-shift

without making
a slip

like calling a rod
a snake

a calf an idol

God is a cash cow

Morning

nameless coffee springs
to the table

behaving like brand *x*
on taste buds where 'is'

differs and drips context
into a translucent cup

since liquid taste
is intimate

dreams as well agitate
to write themselves

down in one gulp
memory, not events

begotten per se

who am I, anyway?

The window back

eyes in the back
of your head

see without reversal
what a rearview sees

the advantage:
you don't

eat with the wrong
hand

Ground zero

a subtle rub
heats denial

its stimulus
as in jumping

you squat deeper
before takeoff

by distance we mean
the collapsible

kaleidoscope
of attention

brushing the present
instance that tells

how to arrive
just here

without the other:
distraction

the *no way*
voiced

in your default setting

A shot in the dark

this gap
where the soul
was said to live

this intractable flash
that surrenders
expectancy

this *now* that
gathersA shot in the dark
and lets go skyward

this open vowel
(inward breath)
pelvis

through which you
arrive at your address
in this world

ah

The call

no space to install
a new

novelty whose promise

to unplump desire
does nothing

at the gas station
a man, shaggy white hair

above a jean jacket,
plops cans from the trash

into a black plastic bag
over one shoulder—

shushing thin metal

angelic voices

The splash

a leaf jumped
ship and danced
before it fell on a puddle

now to cross an item off
its bucket list

and give the smug survivors
a thing to talk about

't' was the *danse macabre*
vainglories of earthly life'

a small shrug
of its thin frail shoulders
at the water's surface

is romantic

Counsel

turn it around

make self-distance
a tide
like a sell-off in the market

and publicizing
might show a sign

to your advantage

that deforms what proves
attractive

a *felix culpa*
the way original sin

is said to make you
more soulful

Verdict

the single star
a late firefly
hopes for fame

whimsy is when
you drop all
pretension
and stop ranking

established reason
a risk

like a shrug
at an offer
of clemency
or dismissal

Message

up and coming
quick wrist flick of revelation

two palms cup
a presence
weak by effort

spring bulbs root under
fall leaves

silent surround

I want to tell you
time
its muscular tic

passes with midges
you swat away

soon no suffering
to boast

Autumn

a blush comes from
the faint lift
arched eyebrows
rolling eyes

a soubrette
sentimental cruelty

but a pink-lined
oak leaf

has bright chemicals
that return love

from enzymes
in flush of need

bounded desire is
a snare that
leaves us thinking

consciousness
is so boring

let's just rake

Solution

the Beasly Boys sing
'Push to ground'

whose riff describes
or prescribes

what is happening
down the passage

through which faith flees
flirting here with

someone's raked
leaf pile dropped

into a culvert
to block the stream

escaping downhill
to the endless sea

Rescue

the Saint Bernard
on a match book cover
says Buffalo New York

over a zip code

no matches light,
a local news report

signs of the times
often is an ill-paid prompt

requiring parody
to give sense

otherwise being bent
to cling cleaves
the literal mind

subject to
mass hysteria

and doesy-dos

Prescience

the third eye
on a dollar bill

sees our felt distance
from a deposed past

as collectible

it sees
the trickle

of art
(really, scribble-throughs)

but lacks the umph
to win the right

vote—
how much is it worth?

Faith

'Life is short'
on a Gainesville
megachurch sign

don't slip
wear rubber soles

look all ways
before you cross

use a lamp
avoid SAD collapse

we're made up of
tiny rules

that follow themselves
or try

in truth
quiet kills us

we depend on
our itches

to blind us
to the ample

time given
for just living

forget why
life lives

Medley

'must win'
sign on heaven's gate

meet those elected
new souls

as backwash of
revelation

hear seraphim cheep
reserve space

. . . . .

triumph is
synonymous with
increased

input
influence is
God

. . . . .

necessity mothers
parsing

leaves
littering the lawn

each feeling
obedient to loll

. . . . .

belief is the loss
we suffer

when seeming flees

Danse

crystals, gelid, luminous
mock the letter K
scratched on glass

between slats of Venetian
blinds

a ballerina
holding a split

hurtles and fidgets
a spotlight
out of empty space

that asks not to be
recognized

as a monograph
is too faded
to identify

the enormous talent
of engraviture

Care-giving

a lone house wren
does its pensum
under a plastic feeder

afterthought:
refuse to absolve

hunger, its clairvoyance
stretches past
to cast out devils

of hope

since I have extra seed

for a pair of mourning doves
on a high-rise branch—
study of patience

as in thinking
everything sparkles
and then doesn't

Reproduction

small brown spider
pushes egg sac
up a windowpane

outside: her aim
to be the sun

put winter on ice

she's part way up
speaking of herself
to herself

arachnid phonemes
fall like skips

a refrain
to herself
for scheming

light
she utters speech

like altitude

it's the weave
a god would knit

On tour

the rakish tittle
of trashcans in snow

explains a future
(to not be sentimental)

that chose danger
of being amused

slowly unfolding
a bus tour map

double-marked in
plastic greens and blues

where what to avoid
is overwritten

which is to say
bound to happen

repeating
the perverse grin

on a con-artist
who makes a face

at the kitchen window
taking garbage out

over my cup of coffee.

In praise

trees are set
to glaze over argument

the big picture
glitteringly obscure

things muffled
beautifully remote

ice on the volar side
husbands the bark

while distally is raw
consisting of a thousand

pearls of need
do not make a list

of sense—
all praise to ice

tacked on
to shape

contingency
alters a mood

as if to mint
treacherous still-born

life

Afterlife

does the sun really
have rays (radii)

above us before us
eternally to set

in glints we can't
conceive

glancing off
the face of delight

like a Farmers' Almanac
sketch

warming chilling freezing
a barren house

where the soul was believed
to live

and go 'where'?

Getaway

'they bought two air tickets'
punch line, no joke

. . .

it's complex
an empty vitamin bottle
at the bottom

of my winter trash basket
wants to be looked after

at my eco-pleasure
how many things are alike
with desire expired?

. . .

a smile in snow
on a ridge-pole at the studio

is erotic

wily cloned chaos

Duotrope

to speak to snowflakes
no, it's an aerator

oil thick with cold
playing castaway
on a sound stage

the sound-alike
of someone walking
on your grave

casts out a real flesh
and blood devil
that's conjured a storm

the two—nature and
culture—vie
for radio audiences

with pings by which
to find a lost object

as it comes to relation
in an alien body

you hope it's yours
(leaving out the wobble)

do you now return
the misread message?

Artistry

think of ghost impresarios
who manhandle
a foist of oak trees

stacked for a cancan

with 1940s pinup girls
in Brownie uniforms

I've moved to a mouse
(this can happen)

that redraws lines
into a cartoon

widely available in
public shelters

where a wry face
brings a sigh

as well as love
of geometry

does it mean I can survive
death?

The news

endgame for imaging
Rover lands on Mars

rock looks like rock

it was our understanding
that things would be
stippled

faded

the way nostalgia works
a honeycomb of canals

plied by bogeymen
in Venetian hats

but no, there next to it
lolling on the horizon

an ancient Coca-Cola truck

www.ingramcontent.com/pod-product-compliance
Lightning Source LLC
LaVergne TN
LVHW090126160826
845673LV00015B/1037

* 9 7 8 8 1 1 9 2 2 8 1 4 0 *